31 DAYS of JESUS SAYINGS

31 Days of Jesus Sayings:
Pocket Edition

Copyright © 2016, 2023
Stephen Joseph Wolf
All rights reserved.
No part of this book may be copied or reproduced in any form or by any means without the written permission of the publisher, except for the inclusion of brief quotations in a review.

Stephen Joseph Wolf is retired, a former parish priest (22 lents & holy weeks), spiritual director and retreat leader, and former certified public accountant (14 tax seasons), and before that worked as a landscaper, desk clerk, laundry worker, janitor, paper boy, and student.

For more visit **www.idjc.org**.

Printed and distributed by Ingram Books.

ISBN 978-1-937081-47-8

See *A Jesus Breviary* for all 8 in 1.
- 31 Days of God's Love-Call
- 31 Days of Jesus Incarnate
- 31 Days of Jesus Miracles
- 31 Days of Jesus Parables
- 31 Days of Jesus Sayings
- 31 Days of Jesus' Paschal Mystery
- 31 Days of the Holy Spirit
- 31 Days on the Christian Life

and *Rainbow Prayer, Dawn & Dusk Rainbow Prayer,* and *Dawn & Dusk Rainbow Prayer for Ordinary Time*

31 DAYS *of* **JESUS SAYINGS**

(an incomplete list,
most from Sunday readings)

Many good people have written books with titles such as *The Life of Jesus* or *A Life of Christ*. This is not one of those.

In addition to the four canonical or church-sanctioned gospels of *Matthew*, *Mark*, *Luke* and *John*, there are other books called *gospels* from near ancient times, and some folks have composed even to recent years accounts of the *evangelion* or *good news* of Jesus Christ. It could even be an instructive exercise for a modern Christian to write out how he or she might tell the story of the Baptism of the Lord, his three-year ministry of teaching and healing, his Passion and death on the cross, and his Resurrection and Ascension. (See Acts 1:22 for how this capacity might qualify one to be an *apostle*.) But this is not one of those.

Scripture scholars have identified a number of passages that can be found in both *Matthew* and *Luke* which are not in either *Mark* or *John*. Based on the most commonly accepted notion of how the gospels were written: *Mark*, perhaps around the year 75(?), from oral traditions; *Matthew* and *Luke*, perhaps around the mid-80's; and *John*, perhaps in the 90's; that each of the four has material in none of the others; that both *Matthew* and *Luke* relied heavily on *Mark*; and that there is matching material in *Matthew* and *Luke* which is not in *Mark* or in *John*, so a theory has evolved that there was a long-lost collection of *Sayings of Jesus*, or a *gospel* often called "Q" after the German word *Quelle* or "source," which both *Matthew* and *Luke* seem to have put to good use. Many have composed possible lists of these sayings of Jesus. This is not one of those.

So what is this? It is simply a meditation rendering of words attributed to Jesus by the writers of the gospels that one parish priest has found helpful in praying *Lectio Divina*, while walking in the woods or on a treadmill or other torture device, driving here and there, or rocking in a chair like a hungry old bear. Nothing more.

There could be many ways to use a collection such as this:

a. One a day for the 31 days of a month, like a vitamin.

b. Choosing a saying or a phrase to pray, and breathing with it through the day.

c. Wanting an introduction to this Jesus of Nazareth.

d. Searching for some healing words of consolation.

e. Being open to a message of challenge from the Loving Savior.

f. A doorway into the gospel context of a saying that intrigues.

g. The ongoing search for
   the gospel account or parable that is
   "the gospel within the gospels" for me.

h. With extra time on my hands,
   finally getting around to sitting with
   those "hard" sayings of Jesus.

i. A way to begin a new dialogue
   with Christ the Lord.

j. Admitting the desire to be
   a disciple of the Master Teacher.

k. Looking to listen to God in patient
   anticipation of a surprise.

I hope you find this meditation rendering of some sayings of Jesus helpful. Take a pencil to them, and if you are convinced any of these are simply wrong, or if any critical sayings are missing, I welcome your input. All God blessings.

Steve Wolf
idjc.org

1

(in the temple at the age of 12)

Why did you look for me?
Did you not know I would be
in the household of my Abba?
Luke 2:49

(about the age of 30 when
John hesitates to baptize Jesus)

This is fitting for us to fulfill all that is right.
Matthew 3:15

(in the desert)

It has been written,
Not on bread alone shall the human live.
Luke 4:4

It has been written,
*You shall worship the Lord your God
and only your God shall you serve.*
Luke 4:8

It has been written,
You shall not test the Lord your God.
Luke 4:12

2

(to two of John's disciples
now following him)

What do you seek?
John 1:38

(when they ask where he stays)

Come, and you will see.
John 1:39

(in Cana)

Fill the water pots with water...
Draw and carry some
to the master of the feast.
John 2:7,8

(in Capernaum at Galilee)

The time is full
and the reign of God has drawn near;
repent - convert - let your heart be changed
and believe in the gospel.
Mark 1:15

3

(in Nazareth)

*The Spirit of the Lord is upon me;
the Lord anointed me
to bring good news to the poor
and sent me
to proclaim release to captives,
sight to the blind,
and freedom to the oppressed,
to proclaim
a year of the Lord's acceptance.*
Luke 4:18; Isaiah 61:1,2; 58:6

Today this scripture is fulfilled
in your hearing.
Luke 4:21

No prophet is acceptable in the native place.
Luke 4:24

(in Capernaum, to an unclean spirit)

Be quiet, and come out from him.
Luke 4:35

Come after me
and I will make you fishers of human beings.
Matthew 4:19

4

(in Capernaum at Galilee)

Let me preach also in the villages near.
Mark 1:38

(To the Leper who said, *If you are willing you are able to cleanse me*)

I am willing; be cleansed.
Mark 1:41

Is it easier to say to the paralytic,
your sins are forgiven,
or to say, rise and walk?
That you may know
that the Son of humanity
has authority to forgive sins on earth,
to you paralyzed I say,
rise,
take your mat,
and go to your house.
Mark 2:9-11

New wine is put into fresh wineskins.
Mark 2:22

5

The Sabbath was made for human beings,
not human beings for the Sabbath.
Mark 2:27

The Son of humanity
is Lord also of the Sabbath.
Mark 2:28

If a house be divided against itself
that house will be unable to stand.
Mark 3:25

Whoever does the will of God
is my brother and sister and mother.
Mark 3:35

To the one who has, more will be given;
from the one who has not,
even what that one has will be taken away.
Mark 4:25

The Reign of God is as when
a human might throw the seed on the earth
and sleep and rise night and day
and the seed sprouts and grows
without the human knowing it.
Mark 4:26,27

6

Who touched my garments?
Mark 5:30

Talitha koum,
little girl I say to you, arise.
Mark 5:41

Take nothing on the way
except only a staff,
sandals, and a single tunic.
Mark 6:8,9

Come yourselves privately
to a desert place
and rest a little.
Mark 6:31

There is nothing entering from outside
that can defile a human;
rather things that defile
come from within.
Mark 7:15

Ephphatha! You be opened.
Mark 7:34

7

Who do people say I am?
Who do you say I am?
Mark 8:27,29

The Son of humanity
will be betrayed into human hands
and they will kill him
and three days after being killed
he will rise up.
Mark 9:31

If anyone wishes to be first
that one shall be last of all
and servant of all.
Mark 9:35

Whoever receives me
receives the One who sent me.
Mark 9:37b

Whoever gives you to drink
a cup of water
because you are of Christ
will not lose that one's reward.
Mark 9:41

8

Allow the children to come to me
and do not prevent them,
for of such is the reign of God.
Mark 10:14

Amen I tell you, whoever does not
receive the reign of God as a child
by no means may enter into it.
Mark 10:15

Go, sell what things you have
and give to the poor
and you will have treasure in heaven,
and come follow me.
Mark 10:21

It is easier for a camel
to go through the eye of a needle
than for one who is rich
to enter into the reign of God.
Mark 10:25

With humans it is impossible
but not with God,
for all things are possible with God.
Mark 10:27

9

Even the Son of humanity
did not come to be served but to serve,
to give his life in ransom for the many.
Mark 10:45

(to blind Bartimaeus)
What do you wish me to do for you?
...Go, your faith has healed you.
Mark 10:51,52

The first:
*Hear, Israel, the Lord our God is One
and you shall love the Lord your God
with all your heart, with all your soul
with all your mind, & with all your strength.*
The second is this:
You shall love your neighbor as yourself.
No commandment is greater than these.
Mark 12:29-31

This widow out of her poverty put in all
things, how much she had, all of her living.
Mark 12:44

Heaven and earth will pass away
but my words will not pass away.
Mark 13:31

10

Blessed are the poor in spirit
for theirs is the reign of heaven.
Matthew 5:3

Blessed are the ones mourning
for they will be comforted.
Matthew 5:4

Blessed are the meek
for they will inherit the earth.
Matthew 5:5

Blessed are those hungering and thirsting
for what is right; they will be satisfied.
Matthew 5:6

Blessed are the merciful
for they will obtain mercy.
Matthew 5:7

Blessed are the clean of heart
for they will see God.
Matthew 5:8

Blessed are the peacemakers for they
will be called sons and daughters of God.
Matthew 5:9

11

Blessed are those persecuted for what is right
for theirs is the reign of heaven.
Matthew 5:10

Blessed are you when they disrespect,
persecute, and tell all the lies against you
for my sake; rejoice and be glad
for great is your reward in heaven.
Matthew 5:11,12a

You are the salt of the earth.
You are the light of the cosmos.
Matthew 5:13,14

Let the light of you shine before humanity
that they may see your good works
and give glory to your Abba in heaven.
Matthew 5:16

I come not to destroy the law
or the prophets but to fulfill.
Matthew 5:17

Whoever does and teaches these
commandments will be called great
in the reign of heaven.
Matthew 5:19b

12

You have heard it said
an eye for an eye and a tooth for a tooth
but I tell you, do not resist an evil doer.
Matthew 5:38,39

To one who strikes you on the right cheek
turn the other as well.
Matthew 5:39b

If someone wishes to sue you to get
your tunic let that one take also the cloak.
When someone forces you to go one mile
go with them for two.
When someone asks you to give
or wants to borrow from you,
do not turn that one away.
Matthew 5:40,41,42

When you do almsgiving,
let not your left hand know
what your right hand does.
Matthew 6:3

When you pray,
enter your room and close your door
and pray to your Abba in secret.
Matthew 6:6

13

Where your treasure is
there also will your heart be.
Matthew 6:21

Look at the birds of heaven and see;
they do not sow or reap or gather into barns
and your heavenly Abba feeds them.
Matthew 6:26

Do not worry about tomorrow
for tomorrow will worry about itself;
sufficient to the day is its own trouble.
Matthew 6:34

Do not judge, lest you be judged.
Matthew 7:1

As you wish for humans to do to you
so also do to them;
this is the law and the prophets.
Matthew 7:12

Everyone who hears my words
and does them
will be like a wise human
who built the house on the rock.
Matthew 7:24

14

Ones who are well
have no need of a physician but the sick do.
I came not to call the righteous but sinners.
Matthew 9:12,13b

Go and learn this,
I desire mercy and not sacrifice.
Matthew 9:13a, 12:7, Hosea 6:6

Go to the lost sheep.
Matthew 10:6

Heal the ill, raise the dead,
cleanse lepers, throw out demons;
freely you have received, so freely give.
Matthew 10:8

Be not afraid of ones who can kill the body
but are unable to kill the soul.
Fear only the One able to destroy
both soul and body in gehenna.
Matthew 10:28

(and)

Be not afraid.

words said to appear in the Bible 365 times

15

One loving abba or momma or son or
daughter more than me is not worthy of me.
Matthew 10:37

Who does not take his or her cross
and follow after me is not worthy of me.
Matthew 10:38

One finding ones own life will lose it
and one losing one's life for my sake
will find it.
Matthew 10:39

I give thanks to you Abba,
Lord of heaven and earth,
who have hidden these things
from the wise and the learned
and revealed them to little ones.
Matthew 11:25

Come to me
all who labor and are burdened,
and I will rest you;
my yoke is gentle
and my burden is light.
Matthew 11:28-30

16

Blessed are your eyes for they see
and your ears for they hear
what many prophets and just ones
longed to see and hear.
Matthew 13:16,17a

That sown on the good soil is the one
hearing and understanding the word
who indeed bears fruit.
Matthew 13:23

Leave both the weeds and the wheat
to grow together until the harvest.
Matthew 13:30

The reign of heaven is like
mustard grain a human sows in the field,
the smallest of the seeds
that grows into the largest garden plant and
becomes a tree where the birds of the sky
can come and dwell in its branches.
Matthew 13:31,32

The reign of heaven is like leaven
a woman mixes into three measures of flour
until the whole is leavened.
Matthew 13:33

17

The reign of heaven is like
a treasure hidden in a field
which a human finds and hides
and in joy goes and sells everything
and buys that field.
Matthew 13:44

The reign of heaven is like
a merchant seeking fine pearls,
who finds one precious pearl
and going away sells everything and buys it.
Matthew 13:45,46

Every scribe discipled
to the reign of heaven
is like a head of a household
who puts forth from the treasure
things both new and old.
Matthew 13:52

Take courage; it is me. Come.
Matthew 14:27,29

Little-faith, why did you doubt?
Matthew 14:31

18

(to the Canaanite woman)
Woman, great is your faith;
let it be done as you desire.
Matthew 15:28

What is the profit for a human to
gain the whole world but lose his or her life?
Matthew 16:26

Where two or three are gathered
in my name there am I in the midst of them.
Matthew 18:20

I tell you, forgive, not seven times
but to seventy times seven.
Matthew 18:22

Forgive each brother and sister
from your heart.
Matthew 18:35

The tax collectors and prostitutes are going
into the reign of God before you.
Matthew 21:31

Go to the intersections
and as many as you find call to the feast.
Matthew 22:9

19

Whose image and title are on the coin?
Render then to Caesar the things of Caesar
and to God the things of God.
Matthew 22:20, 21

Scribes and Pharisees preach
and do not do it;
they put on human shoulders
heavy burdens bound
but are unwilling
to lift a finger to move them.
Matthew 23:3b,4

The greatest of you will be your servant.
Matthew 23:11

Watch ready,
for you know neither the day nor the hour.
Matthew 25:13

I was hungry and you gave me to eat
thirsty and you gave me drink
a stranger and you welcomed me
naked and you clothed me
ill and you cared for me
in prison and you came to me.
Matthew 25:35,36

20

Put out into the deep
and let down your nets for a catch.
Luke 5:4

I have come to call not the righteous
but sinners to conversion.
Luke 5:32

Blessed are you poor
for yours is the reign of God.
Luke 6:20b

Blessed are you hungering now
for you will be satisfied.
Luke 6:21a

Blessed are you weeping now
for you will laugh.
Luke 6:21b

Blessed are you when humans hate you
and exclude you and reproach you
and kick out your name as evil
for the sake of the Son of humanity.
Luke 6:22

21

Rejoice on that day and leap for joy
for great is your reward in heaven.
Luke 6:23

To you hearing I say, love your enemies
and do good to the ones hating you.
Luke 6:27

Be merciful as your Abba is merciful.
Luke 6:36

Give and it will be given to you;
the measure you measure
will be measured to you.
Luke 6:38

Can a blind one guide one who is blind?
Will not both fall into a ditch?
Luke 6:39

Why do you see
the piece of dust in your neighbor's eye
but ignore the wood beam
in your own eye?
Luke 6:41

Young human, I say to you, arise!
Luke 7:14

22

Do you see this woman?
Her many sins have been forgiven
and so she has loved much.
Luke 7:44,47

The seed is the word of God.
Luke 8:11b

Give them food yourselves.
Luke 9:13

Get the people to recline
in groups of about fifty.
Luke 9:14

If anyone wishes to come after me
let that one deny the self
take daily his or her cross and follow me.
Luke 9:23

Whoever is not against you is for you.
Luke 9:50

Foxes have holes
and birds of the sky have nests
but the Son of humanity has no place
where his head may lay.
Luke 9:58

23

Leave the dead to bury their own dead;
you go proclaim the reign of God.
Luke 9:60

The harvest is plenty but workers are few;
ask the Lord of the harvest
to throw workers into the harvest.
Luke 10:2

(As the Samaritan did mercy to the beaten man)

You go and do likewise.
Luke 10:37

Ask and it will be given you,
seek and you will find,
knock and it will be opened to you.
Luke 11:9

If you know
to give good gifts to your children
how much more will the heavenly Abba
give the Holy Spirit to those who ask.
Luke 11:13

Be wary and on guard against all greed
for life is not about possessions.
Luke 12:15

24

I have come to throw fire on the earth
and how I wish it was ablaze.
Luke 12:49

There are last ones who will be first
and first ones who will be last.
Luke 13:30

Jerusalem, Jerusalem,
how often have I wished
to gather your children
as a hen does her brood under her wings.
Luke 13:34

When you are invited, take the lowest place;
one exalting the self will be humbled
and one humbling the self will be exalted.
Luke 14:10,11

Any of you who do not detach from
all your possessions cannot be my disciple.
Luke 14:33

Joy in heaven over one sinner converting
will exceed that over ninety-nine
of the righteous with no need of conversion.
Luke 15:7

25

No servant can serve two lords
and so you cannot serve God and mammon.
Luke 16:13

If you had faith as a mustard grain
you would have said to this mulberry tree
be uprooted and planted in the sea
and it would have obeyed you.
Luke 17:6

When you do all things commanded say, *we
unprofitable servants have done as obliged.*
Luke 17:10

Were not ten lepers cleansed? And this
one foreigner alone gives glory to God?
Luke 17:17,18

But when the Son of humanity comes
will he find faith on earth?
Luke 18:8

The tax collector standing far off
would not lift his eyes to heaven
but beat his breast saying,
'God, be merciful to me, a sinner.'
Luke 18:13

26

Zacchaeus, come down quickly
for this day it is fitting
for me to stay at your house.
Luke 19:5

The Son of humanity came
to seek and to save the lost.
Luke 19:10

The Lord is God of the living.
Luke 20:38

I will give you a mouth and wisdom
that will not be contradicted or withstood.
Luke 21:15

You will be with me in paradise.
Luke 23:43

You are witnesses of these things,
the Christ to suffer
and rise on the third day.
Luke 24:46

27

As wind blows where it wishes
and you hear it not knowing
where it comes from
or where it goes
so is everyone who is born of the Spirit.
John 3:8

God so loved the cosmos,
and so gave the only begotten Son
that everyone believing in him
may not perish but have life eternal.
John 3:16

The one doing the truth
comes to the light.
John 3:21

My food is that I may do
the will of the one who sent me.
John 4:34

Do you want to be whole?
John 5:6

Gather the fragments left over
so that nothing is lost.
John 6:12

28

Work not for food that perishes
but for the food that endures to life eternal
which the Son of humanity gives you.
John 6:27a

I am the bread of life;
who comes to me does not hunger
and who believes in me will never thirst.
John 6:35

I am the living bread from heaven; anyone
who eats of this bread will live to the eon.
John 6:51a

The bread that I will give
is my flesh for the life of the cosmos.
John 6:51b

Let whoever thirsts come to me and drink.
John 7:37

Let the one of you without sin
be first to throw a stone.
John 8:7

I am the light of the cosmos.
John 8:12b

29

When he sends forth all his own
he goes before them and the sheep follow
because they know his voice.
John 10:4

I came that they may have life
and to the full.
John 10:10b

I am the good shepherd
and I know mine and mine know me.
John 10:14

The Abba and I are one.
John 10:30

Unless the grain of wheat
falling to the ground dies
it remains one grain,
but if it dies it bears much fruit.
John 12:24

Whoever serves me the Abba will honor.
John 12:26b

When I am lifted up from the earth
I will draw everyone to myself.
John 12:32

30

As I the Lord and Teacher washed your feet
so are you to wash the feet of each other.
John 13:14

Do not let your hearts be troubled...
I am the way and the truth and the life.
John 14:1,6a

Anyone who loves me will keep my word;
my Abba will love that one within whom
we will come to make our dwelling.
John 14:23

The Holy Spirit, the Paraclete,
will teach you all things.
John 14:26

I am the true vine
and my Abba is the grower.
John 15:1

Love one another as I have loved you.
...I have called you friends.
John 15:12,15b

I have much more to tell you
but you cannot bear it yet.
John 16:12

31

When coming, the Spirit of truth
will guide you into all truth.
John 16:13

Do you ask if I am a ruler from yourself
or have others told you about me?
John 18:34

Peace to you; as the Abba has sent me,
so I send you; receive the Holy Spirit.
John 20:21

Whose sins you forgive, they are forgiven;
whose sins you hold, they are held.
John 20:23

Do you believe because you have seen me?
Blessed are those not seeing but believing.
John 20:29

Go into all the cosmos
and proclaim the gospel to all creation.
Mark 16:15

Behold, I am with you always
until the completion of the eons.
Matthew 28:20

www.ingramcontent.com/pod-product-compliance
Lightning Source LLC
Chambersburg PA
CBHW021200080526
44588CB00008B/434